THE WASTE LAND AND OTHER POEMS
Celebrating One Hundred Years of The Waste Land

THE WASTE LAND AND OTHER POEMS

Celebrating One Hundred Years of The Waste Land

T. S. Eliot

BLACK EAGLE BOOKS
Dublin, USA | BBSR, India

Black Eagle Books
USA address:
7464 Wisdom Lane
Dublin, OH 43016

India address:
E/312, Trident Galaxy, Kalinga Nagar,
Bhubaneswar-751003, Odisha, India

E-mail: info@blackeaglebooks.org
Website: www.blackeaglebooks.org

First International Edition Published by
Black Eagle Books, 2022

THE WASTE LAND AND OTHER POEMS
by T. S. Eliot

Cover & Interior Design: Ezy's Publication

ISBN- 978-1-64560-342-9 (Paperback)

Printed in the United States of America

Contents

INTRODUCTION

A few months ago, in 2022, a six-day festival called FRAGMENTS was organised in London to mark the 100 years of The Waste Land by TS Eliot, arguably the greatest poet of the twentieth century. The festival featured multiple diverse performances in 22 of the most beautiful and extraordinarily intimate late-medieval churches of London. The City of London was selected on the basis of the actual geography of the poem's setting that had inspired Eliot's haunting vision of a collapsing European culture. Each fragment was performed in a location that created an intimate connection between the poem and the place.

Celebration of the 100th anniversary of The Waste Land was not confined to London alone, it was celebrated all over the English-speaking literary world, including India. The Society for the Study of the Multi-Ethnic Literatures of the World (MELOW) organised a three-day International Conference at Goa to celebrate the 100th anniversary of the great work, one of the forbiddingly difficult and complex works of "high modernism" of the twentieth century.

Ramadevi Women's University of Bhubaneswar and Ravenshaw University of Cuttack, apart from some government and non-government colleges of the Indian state of Odisha organised seminars in honour of The Waste Land. Discussion on The Waste Land focused on how the modernist masterpiece had baffled and moved readers for a century with its great innovative power. The professor seminarists discussed the modes of Eliot's reception in India with special reference to Odia, and the overwhelming influence of The Waste Land in particular, on a new generation of Odia poets, who forged a new idiom to break away from the cramping romantic Sabuja tradition of poetry writing. As a matter of fact, it was Eliot who had greatly affected Odia poetry that looked upon him as the messiah of a "new" movement.

Widely regarded as "The Poem of the Century, "The Waste Land is an "infinitely mysterious poem," which, according to John Xiron Cooper, "is a poem we have learned to handle, but not a poem, we have tamed." It is true that publication of the poem marked a watershed moment in the history of British poetry. Soon after its appearance, first in the inaugural volume of The Criterion (October 1922), a quarterly British literary magazine, founded and edited by Eliot himself, in London, and next in the American publication The Dial in New York (November 1922), the poem came to be regarded as one of the seminal works of modernist poetry, and Eliot as a very important literary figure of the time. Eliot earned the Dial Award of $2,000

Like other long poems, The Waste Land was composed over a substantial period and appeared in its final form with end-notes. The five-part poem was dedicated to Ezra Pound, his friend and mentor whom he referred to as il miglior fabbro meaning "a better craftsman." Pound played a major role in the success of the poem by trimming down a sprawling, chaotic manuscript of over 800 lines to just 433 lines. Once Eliot said of his friend and mentor, "Mr. Pound is more responsible for the 20th-century revolution in poetry than any other individual." Eliot was always grateful to the better craftsman not because of his act of condensation but for what he called 'maieutic' endeavour.

Widely regarded as "The Poem of the Century," The Waste Land expressed concerns not only about the collapse of Western civilisation, but the modern people's spiritual barrenness, which may be interpreted from numerous different perspectives. Despite the fact that it is a notoriously difficult poem, various critics have adopted different approaches to understand the poem, its extensive use of allusions, monologues, dialogues and free speech, its articulation of different voices, and changing styles. Yet, soon after its publication in Britain and America, The Waste Land set off a critical firestorm in the literary world. It generated the most violent literary controversy of the century. Many readers, critics and intellectuals were shocked to read Eliot's text in which he had painted the modern world characterised by experiences of deep despair and gruesome disillusionment.

The lack of unified theme and coherent structure, its polyglottal allusions encouraged the critics to denounce the work in no uncertain terms. The Time magazine branded the poem a "hoax". Highly critical of Eliot, William Carlos Williams, an American poet and writer stated that he disliked The Waste Land because it 'returned us to the classroom.' And "It wiped out our world as if an atom bomb had been dropped upon it..." According to F. R.

Leavis, the poem showed us "a rich disorganization," and a "vision of desolation and spiritual drought." Cleanth Brooks called it "a sigh for the vanished glory of the past."

It was a time, when according to St Bernard, life seemed almost impossible to live in, a world that was marked by pain, death and suffering. It was like "a misery to be born and a trouble to die." The Waste Land captured the mood of the time in such an elusive manner that it became outrageously impenetrable to readers. They considered The Waste Land to be Eliot's forbiddingly complex work that used a technique which was bewilderingly modernist. Yet many readers hailed the poem as a masterpiece that exercised a mesmerising effect on their minds. IA Richards, the famous British critic, had all praise for Eliot for reflecting succinctly the post-war "sense of desolation, of uncertainty, of futility, of the groundlessness of aspirations, of the vanity of endeavour, and a thirst for a life-giving water which seems suddenly to have failed." But Eliot was not happy the way Richards described the situation. He did not agree to what Richards said that he had expressed "the disillusionment of a generation," which, according to Eliot, was sheer nonsense. He asserted how it was not part of his intention.

It is important to note that The Waste Land has no definite structure. It is a poem that does not have a plot. Nor does it have a beginning nor an end. The poetic fragments mirror the fragmentation of life in the cities of Europe, devastated by World War I. It can be termed as "a heap of broken images," a poem, as asserted by Harold Munro, "a potpourri of descriptions and episodes." Since the poem is based on Tiresias's visions which come to him in spurts, The Waste Land seems to be fragmented or disjointed. The reader is expected to string all these fragments together to derive meaning.

The Waste Land is also a multi-voiced poem, it has a multitude of voices, voices spoken in Greek, Latin, Sanskrit, German, and Italian. It is also richly allusive and polyvocal. It alludes to several texts such as Ovid's Metamorphoses, Dante's Divine Comedy, Baudelaire's Les Fleurs du mal, Shakespeare, Buddhism, Hindu Upanishad and others. The mind-boggling allusiveness and profundity of the text just went over the heads of his readers, who were initially baffled by a string of quotations and reference to a variety of sources in multiple languages like Greek, Latin, French, German, Italian and Sanskrit. They could hardly grasp Eliot's 'aesthetics' of fragmentation and juxtaposition, which can be taken as an inextricable part of the poem's symbolic significance.

The Waste Land derives its theme from the two scholarly works of the time: Jessie L Weston's From Ritual to Romance (1920) and Sir James George Frazer's The Golden Bough: A Study in Magic in Religion (1890) which, according to Eliot, had "influenced our generation profoundly." Miss Weston's book had been hailed as a landmark of anthropological and mythological scholarship in which she explores how medieval romances like the Grail legends can be traced back to fertility rites. Weston recounts the Grail legend in which the central hero, the Knight Perceval, goes through a terrible ordeal of a desolate wasteland in order to attain the vision of the Grail. The vision would help him heal the impotent Fisher King who has been wounded and maimed through both his thighs by a javelin in the battlefield. The magic wound of the Fisher King resulting in his sexual impotence wilts his kingdom into a wasteland. The kingdom looks arid and desolate, and not even a blade of grass grows there. The Fisher King is so named because he chooses to spend his time angling with a hook on the river near his castle. The knight Perceval eventually comes to the castle of the Fisher King in search of the Holy Grail.

The multi-volume The Golden Bough in which Frazer makes a highly influential anthropological study of myth traces the connections between mythology and religion. Eliot uses Frazer's images of death and resurrection, dying or reviving in order to emphasise the endless spiritual vacuity of his times. Eliot uses "mythical method," a modernist technique of bringing out a qualitative parallelism between the past and the present, and "manipulating a continuous parallel between antiquity and contemporaneity." As Eliot stated in his review of James Joyce's Ulysses, it is "a way of controlling, or ordering, of giving a shape and a significance to the immense panorama of futility and anarchy which is contemporary history." The story of the Fisher King who sits fishing in his barren kingdom, guarding the Holy Grail is a part of fertility myth that Eliot uses as theme of The Waste Land. In Eliot's Notes, the Prophet Tiresias, an ancient blind Greek seer, who is historically connected with the story of King Oedipus of Thebes, is described as "a mere spectator and not indeed a 'character', yet the most important personage in the poem, uniting all the rest." And "What Tiresias sees, in fact, is the substance of the poem." Tiresias has been incorporated into the text as the central character or protagonist of the poem not merely for acquiring a dual-gendered experience, both as male and female, but because he played a very crucial role in fusing different times and places and genders.

The Waste Land is basically a peopled landscape;

many characters, several of whom are women, roam around freely in the wasteland. It is interesting to note that "all the women are one woman, and the two sexes meet in Tiresias." All these women have their own individual story to narrate, their own voice for people to listen to. Such women like Marie, a niece and confidante of Empress Elisabeth of Austria, Belladonna, the Lady of the Rocks, Lil, the mother-of-five whose unhappy marriage is discussed by her friend in a London pub, the fortune-teller Madame Sosostris, the typist girl, who is "bored and tired," the nymphs, who happened to be the friends of the loitering heirs of city directors vary from each other in terms of their age, class, educational level or socio-economic status.

The Waste Land is fragmented into five sections: 'The Burial of the Dead,' 'A Game of Chess', 'The Fire Sermon,' 'Death by Water' and 'What the Thunder Said.'

The first section 'The Burial of the Dead' is derived from the Anglican burial service, and it dwells upon various themes of despair and disillusionment. It begins with a reference to April, which as Eliot believes, is "the cruellest month." It is because Europe had already become a place of hopeless decay and death in the wake of World War I. It was when Eliot was recuperating from nervous breakdown himself, in the peak of marital discord. Spring which is otherwise a season of new life and renewal has turned out to be lifeless and cruel. Again, spring which is supposed to bring back life and activity to all objects of nature remains dead and inactive. Human beings appeared to be happy and joyful in winter: "Winter kept us warm," meaning that winter stood for a life of comfort, of physical joy when the spiritual and moral values are dead and forgotten.

In this section there is an allusion to the "Unreal

City," London, that is described as ugly, cruel and gray which lacks any real human warmth. It represents loss and brokenness, the social, psychological, and emotional collapse which the European people experienced in the wake of the World War I. Eliot like Baudelaire perceived the city as blatantly hostile to their hopes and aspirations, or as creating a depressingly squalid environment in which they feel utterly lonely and sad. Being a pioneer of city poetry Eliot made the "unreal" hallucinatory city as an expression of urban experience.

The second section 'A Game of Chess' refers to Jacobean dramatist Thomas Middleton's two significant plays such as Women Beware Men and A Game of Chess. There is also a reference to Shakespeare's Antony and Cleopatra. Eliot describes a lavishly decorated room in which a woman is seen sitting on a throne-like chair, echoing Shakespeare's "The barge she sat in, like a burnished throne ..."

In 'The Fire Sermon,' the longest section of The Waste Land Eliot alludes to Lord Buddha who delivered a fire sermon on liberating oneself from suffering through the practice of detachment. While addressing a gathering of monks Lord Buddha said, "Everything, monks, is burning...It is burning with the fire of passion, the fire of hatred, the fire of delusion. I declare that it is burning with the fire of birth, decay, death, grief, lamentation, pain, sorrow, and despair." Eliot presents a series of debased sexual encounters that concludes with a river song and a religious encounter.

In the following section, 'The Death by Water,' by far the shortest section of the long poem, the poet tells the story of Phlebes, a young and handsome Phoenician sailor and businessman, who died, apparently by drowning.

Caught in a whirlpool he "passed the stages of his age and youth." There is no hope that he would be reborn; it is because, being a modern man, he nourished no desire to follow a spiritual path. In this section 'Death by Water,' focus shifts from all-consuming fire to the elements of water. Eliot shows the significance of water as a means of purification and re-birth.

The final section 'What the Thunder Said' is written when Eliot was recovering in Lausanne and writing in a kind of trance. Later he confessed that he did not bother whether he understood what he was writing.

The section is based on the story of an arduous journey undertaken by Knight Perceval and his followers to the "Chapel Perilous" in search of the Holy Grail. The aim was to break the curse of sterility upon the land. There is also a reference to the journey of Christ's two disciples to Emmaus, an ancient town mentioned in the Bible, to verify if Christ was reborn. The hooded person walking by their side turned out to be Jesus Christ who was there to convince his followers that he was resurrected.

The poem ends with a string of disparate fragments, interspersed with a story from the Brihadaranyaka Upanishad. In this Hindu text, all the three descendants of Prajapati (Sanskrit: "Lord of Creatures') – Gods, Men and Demons – approached him for advice. Prajapati uttered one syllable in the sound of the thunder DA three times - DA DA DA - meaning Datta" (give), "Dayadhvam" (be compassionate), and "Damyata" (self-control), three guiding principles for all creatures.

Finally, the poem ends with a Sanskrit word: "Shantih," which is repeated thrice "Shantih, Shantih," Shantih" at a stretch. The word is derived from Indian Upanishad, and it is traditionally chanted at the end of most mantras. The word is repeated thrice as an invocation for peace, or as an expression of one's intense desire or commitment to attain peace in life. Eliot finds "The Peace which passeth understanding" as the English equivalent to Shantih in Sanskrit. But many think that Eliot's definition is utterly vague and incomplete, but this does not mean that Eliot has misrepresented the word. Eliot uses these words to signify that redemption is possible despite all odds. Maybe the world is falling apart, there is emotional and spiritual sterility all around, but there is still some hope for humanity to attain salvation.

- Bhagaban Jaysingh

"Nam Sibyllam quidem Cumis ego ipse oculis meis
vidi in ampulla pendere, et cum illi pueri dicerent:
Σίβυλλα τί θέλεις; respondebat illa: ἀποθανεῖν θέλω."

For Ezra Pound
il miglior fabbro.

I. THE BURIAL OF THE DEAD

APRIL is the cruellest month, breeding
Lilacs out of the dead land, mixing
Memory and desire, stirring
Dull roots with spring rain.
Winter kept us warm, covering   5
Earth in forgetful snow, feeding
A little life with dried tubers.
Summer surprised us, coming over the Starnbergersee
With a shower of rain; we stopped in the colonnade,
And went on in sunlight, into the Hofgarten,   10
And drank coffee, and talked for an hour.
Bin gar keine Russin, stamm' aus Litauen, echt deutsch.
And when we were children, staying at the archduke's,
My cousin's, he took me out on a sled,
And I was frightened. He said, Marie,   15
Marie, hold on tight. And down we went.
In the mountains, there you feel free.
I read, much of the night, and go south in the winter.

What are the roots that clutch, what branches grow
Out of this stony rubbish? Son of man,   20
You cannot say, or guess, for you know only
A heap of broken images, where the sun beats,
And the dead tree gives no shelter, the cricket no relief,

And the dry stone no sound of water. Only
There is shadow under this red rock,   25
(Come in under the shadow of this red rock),
And I will show you something different from either
Your shadow at morning striding behind you
Or your shadow at evening rising to meet you;
I will show you fear in a handful of dust.   30
      Frisch weht der Wind
      Der Heimat zu,
      Mein Irisch Kind,
      Wo weilest du?
"You gave me hyacinths first a year ago;   35
They called me the hyacinth girl."
—Yet when we came back, late, from the Hyacinth garden,
Your arms full, and your hair wet, I could not
Speak, and my eyes failed, I was neither
Living nor dead, and I knew nothing,   40
Looking into the heart of light, the silence.
Öd' und leer das Meer.

Madame Sosostris, famous clairvoyante,
Had a bad cold, nevertheless
Is known to be the wisest woman in Europe,   45
With a wicked pack of cards. Here, said she,
Is your card, the drowned Phoenician Sailor,
(Those are pearls that were his eyes. Look!)
Here is Belladonna, the Lady of the Rocks,
The lady of situations.   50
Here is the man with three staves, and here the Wheel,
And here is the one-eyed merchant, and this card,
Which is blank, is something he carries on his back,
Which I am forbidden to see. I do not find
The Hanged Man. Fear death by water.   55
I see crowds of people, walking round in a ring.
Thank you. If you see dear Mrs. Equitone,

Tell her I bring the horoscope myself:
One must be so careful these days.

Unreal City,   60
Under the brown fog of a winter dawn,
A crowd flowed over London Bridge, so many,
I had not thought death had undone so many.
Sighs, short and infrequent, were exhaled,
And each man fixed his eyes before his feet.   65
Flowed up the hill and down King William Street,
To where Saint Mary Woolnoth kept the hours
With a dead sound on the final stroke of nine.
There I saw one I knew, and stopped him, crying "Stetson!
You who were with me in the ships at Mylae!   70
That corpse you planted last year in your garden,
Has it begun to sprout? Will it bloom this year?
Or has the sudden frost disturbed its bed?
Oh keep the Dog far hence, that's friend to men,
Or with his nails he'll dig it up again!   75
You! hypocrite lecteur!—mon semblable,—mon frère!"

II. A GAME OF CHESS

The Chair she sat in, like a burnished throne,
Glowed on the marble, where the glass
Held up by standards wrought with fruited vines
From which a golden Cupidon peeped out   80
(Another hid his eyes behind his wing)
Doubled the flames of sevenbranched candelabra
Reflecting light upon the table as
The glitter of her jewels rose to meet it,
From satin cases poured in rich profusion;   85
In vials of ivory and coloured glass
Unstoppered, lurked her strange synthetic perfumes,
Unguent, powdered, or liquid—troubled, confused

And drowned the sense in odours; stirred by the air
That freshened from the window, these ascended   90
In fattening the prolonged candle-flames,
Flung their smoke into the laquearia,
Stirring the pattern on the coffered ceiling.
Huge sea-wood fed with copper
Burned green and orange, framed by the coloured stone,95
In which sad light a carvèd dolphin swam.
Above the antique mantel was displayed
As though a window gave upon the sylvan scene
The change of Philomel, by the barbarous king
So rudely forced; yet there the nightingale   100
Filled all the desert with inviolable voice
And still she cried, and still the world pursues,
"Jug Jug" to dirty ears.
And other withered stumps of time
Were told upon the walls; staring forms   105
Leaned out, leaning, hushing the room enclosed.
Footsteps shuffled on the stair,
Under the firelight, under the brush, her hair
Spread out in fiery points
Glowed into words, then would be savagely still.   110

"My nerves are bad to-night. Yes, bad. Stay with me.
Speak to me. Why do you never speak? Speak.
What are you thinking of? What thinking? What?
I never know what you are thinking. Think."
I think we are in rats' alley   115
Where the dead men lost their bones.

"What is that noise?"
                  The wind under the door.
"What is that noise now? What is the wind doing?"
                  Nothing again nothing.   120
                        "Do

You know nothing? Do you see nothing? Do you remember
Nothing?"
    I remember
        Those are pearls that were his eyes.   125
"Are you alive, or not? Is there nothing in your head?"
                 But
O O O O that Shakespeherian Rag—
It's so elegant
So intelligent   130

"What shall I do now? What shall I do?
I shall rush out as I am, and walk the street
With my hair down, so. What shall we do to-morrow?
What shall we ever do?"
        The hot water at ten.   135
And if it rains, a closed car at four.
And we shall play a game of chess,
Pressing lidless eyes and waiting for a knock upon the door.

When Lil's husband got demobbed, I said,
I didn't mince my words, I said to her myself,   140
HURRY UP PLEASE ITS TIME
Now Albert's coming back, make yourself a bit smart.
He'll want to know what you done with that money he gave you
To get yourself some teeth. He did, I was there.
You have them all out, Lil, and get a nice set,   145
He said, I swear, I can't bear to look at you.
And no more can't I, I said, and think of poor Albert,
He's been in the army four years, he wants a good time,
And if you don't give it him, there's others will, I said.
Oh is there, she said. Something o' that, I said.   150
Then I'll know who to thank, she said, and give me a straight look.
HURRY UP PLEASE ITS TIME
If you don't like it you can get on with it, I said,
Others can pick and choose if you can't.

But if Albert makes off, it won't be for lack of telling.   155
You ought to be ashamed, I said, to look so antique.
(And her only thirty-one.)
I can't help it, she said, pulling a long face,
It's them pills I took, to bring it off, she said.
(She's had five already, and nearly died of young George.)   160
The chemist said it would be alright, but I've never been the same.
You are a proper fool, I said.
Well, if Albert won't leave you alone, there it is, I said,
What you get married for if you don't want children?
HURRY UP PLEASE ITS TIME   165
Well, that Sunday Albert was home, they had a hot gammon,
And they asked me in to dinner, to get the beauty of it hot—
HURRY UP PLEASE ITS TIME
HURRY UP PLEASE ITS TIME
Goonight Bill. Goonight Lou. Goonight May. Goonight.170
Ta ta. Goonight. Goonight.
Good night, ladies, good night, sweet ladies, good night, good
night.

III. THE FIRE SERMON

The river's tent is broken: the last fingers of leaf
Clutch and sink into the wet bank. The wind
Crosses the brown land, unheard. The nymphs are departed.   175
Sweet Thames, run softly, till I end my song.
The river bears no empty bottles, sandwich papers,
Silk handkerchiefs, cardboard boxes, cigarette ends
Or other testimony of summer nights. The nymphs are departed.
And their friends, the loitering heirs of city directors;   180
Departed, have left no addresses.
By the waters of Leman I sat down and wept...
Sweet Thames, run softly till I end my song,
Sweet Thames, run softly, for I speak not loud or long.
But at my back in a cold blast I hear   185

The rattle of the bones, and chuckle spread from ear to ear.

A rat crept softly through the vegetation
Dragging its slimy belly on the bank
While I was fishing in the dull canal
On a winter evening round behind the gashouse.   190
Musing upon the king my brother's wreck
And on the king my father's death before him.
White bodies naked on the low damp ground
And bones cast in a little low dry garret,
Rattled by the rat's foot only, year to year.   195
But at my back from time to time I hear
The sound of horns and motors, which shall bring
Sweeney to Mrs. Porter in the spring.
O the moon shone bright on Mrs. Porter
And on her daughter   200
They wash their feet in soda water
Et, O ces voix d'enfants, chantant dans la coupole!

Twit twit twit
Jug jug jug jug jug jug
So rudely forc'd.   205
Tereu

Unreal City
Under the brown fog of a winter noon
Mr Eugenides, the Smyrna merchant
Unshaven, with a pocket full of currants   210
C. i. f. London: documents at sight,
Asked me in demotic French
To luncheon at the Cannon Street Hotel
Followed by a week-end at the Metropole.

At the violet hour, when the eyes and back   215
Turn upward from the desk, when the human engine waits

Like a taxi throbbing waiting,
I Tiresias, though blind, throbbing between two lives,
Old man with wrinkled female breasts, can see
At the violet hour, the evening hour that strives   220
Homeward, and brings the sailor home from sea,
The typist home at tea-time, clears her breakfast, lights
Her stove, and lays out food in tins.
Out of the window perilously spread
Her drying combinations touched by the sun's last rays,   225
On the divan are piled (at night her bed)
Stockings, slippers, camisoles, and stays.
I Tiresias, old man with wrinkled dugs
Perceived the scene, and foretold the rest—
I too awaited the expected guest.   230
He, the young man carbuncular, arrives,
A small house-agent's clerk, with one bold stare,
One of the low on whom assurance sits
As a silk hat on a Bradford millionaire.
The time is now propitious, as he guesses,   235
The meal is ended, she is bored and tired,
Endeavours to engage her in caresses
Which still are unreproved, if undesired.
Flushed and decided, he assaults at once;
Exploring hands encounter no defence;   240
His vanity requires no response,
And makes a welcome of indifference.
(And I Tiresias have foresuffered all
Enacted on this same divan or bed;
I who have sat by Thebes below the wall   245
And walked among the lowest of the dead.)
Bestows one final patronizing kiss,
And gropes his way, finding the stairs unlit…

She turns and looks a moment in the glass,
Hardly aware of her departed lover;   250

Her brain allows one half-formed thought to pass:
"Well now that's done: and I'm glad it's over."
When lovely woman stoops to folly and
Paces about her room again, alone,
She smoothes her hair with automatic hand,   255
And puts a record on the gramophone.

"This music crept by me upon the waters"
And along the Strand, up Queen Victoria Street.
O City City, I can sometimes hear
Beside a public bar in Lower Thames Street,   260
The pleasant whining of a mandoline
And a clatter and a chatter from within
Where fishmen lounge at noon: where the walls
Of Magnus Martyr hold
Inexplicable splendour of Ionian white and gold.   265

The river sweats
Oil and tar
The barges drift
With the turning tide
Red sails   270
Wide
To leeward, swing on the heavy spar.
The barges wash
Drifting logs
Down Greenwich reach   275
Past the Isle of Dogs.
        Weialala leia
        Wallala leialala
Elizabeth and Leicester
Beating oars   280
The stern was formed
A gilded shell
Red and gold

The brisk swell
Rippled both shores   285
South-west wind
Carried down stream
The peal of bells
White towers
        Weialala leia   290
        Wallala leialala

"Trams and dusty trees.
Highbury bore me. Richmond and Kew
Undid me. By Richmond I raised my knees
Supine on the floor of a narrow canoe."   295

"My feet are at Moorgate, and my heart
Under my feet. After the event
He wept. He promised 'a new start.'
I made no comment. What should I resent?"

"On Margate Sands.   300
I can connect
Nothing with nothing.
The broken finger-nails of dirty hands.
My people humble people who expect
Nothing."   305

        la la

To Carthage then I came

Burning burning burning burning
O Lord Thou pluckest me out
O Lord Thou pluckest   310

burning

IV. DEATH BY WATER

Phlebas the Phoenician, a fortnight dead,
Forgot the cry of gulls, and the deep seas swell
And the profit and loss.
         A current under sea   315
Picked his bones in whispers. As he rose and fell
He passed the stages of his age and youth
Entering the whirlpool.
         Gentile or Jew
O you who turn the wheel and look to windward,   320
Consider Phlebas, who was once handsome and tall as you.

V. WHAT THE THUNDER SAID

After the torch-light red on sweaty faces
After the frosty silence in the gardens
After the agony in stony places
The shouting and the crying   325
Prison and place and reverberation
Of thunder of spring over distant mountains
He who was living is now dead
We who were living are now dying
With a little patience   330

Here is no water but only rock
Rock and no water and the sandy road
The road winding above among the mountains
Which are mountains of rock without water
If there were water we should stop and drink   335
Amongst the rock one cannot stop or think
Sweat is dry and feet are in the sand
If there were only water amongst the rock
Dead mountain mouth of carious teeth that cannot spit
Here one can neither stand nor lie nor sit   340

There is not even silence in the mountains
But dry sterile thunder without rain
There is not even solitude in the mountains
But red sullen faces sneer and snarl
From doors of mud-cracked houses
                        If there were water   345
And no rock
If there were rock
And also water
And water
A spring   350
A pool among the rock
If there were the sound of water only
Not the cicada
And dry grass singing
But sound of water over a rock   355
Where the hermit-thrush sings in the pine trees
Drip drop drip drop drop drop drop
But there is no water

Who is the third who walks always beside you?
When I count, there are only you and I together   360
But when I look ahead up the white road
There is always another one walking beside you
Gliding wrapt in a brown mantle, hooded
I do not know whether a man or a woman
—But who is that on the other side of you?   365

What is that sound high in the air
Murmur of maternal lamentation
Who are those hooded hordes swarming
Over endless plains, stumbling in cracked earth
Ringed by the flat horizon only   370
What is the city over the mountains
Cracks and reforms and bursts in the violet air

Falling towers
Jerusalem Athens Alexandria
Vienna London   375
Unreal

A woman drew her long black hair out tight
And fiddled whisper music on those strings
And bats with baby faces in the violet light
Whistled, and beat their wings   380
And crawled head downward down a blackened wall
And upside down in air were towers
Tolling reminiscent bells, that kept the hours
And voices singing out of empty cisterns and exhausted wells.

In this decayed hole among the mountains   385
In the faint moonlight, the grass is singing
Over the tumbled graves, about the chapel
There is the empty chapel, only the wind's home.
It has no windows, and the door swings,
Dry bones can harm no one.   390
Only a cock stood on the roof-tree
Co co rico co co rico
In a flash of lightning. Then a damp gust
Bringing rain
Ganga was sunken, and the limp leaves   395
Waited for rain, while the black clouds
Gathered far distant, over Himavant.
The jungle crouched, humped in silence.
Then spoke the thunder
DA   400
Datta: what have we given?
My friend, blood shaking my heart
The awful daring of a moment's surrender
Which an age of prudence can never retract
By this, and this only, we have existed   405

Which is not to be found in our obituaries
Or in memories draped by the beneficent spider
Or under seals broken by the lean solicitor
In our empty rooms
DA   410
Dayadhvam: I have heard the key
Turn in the door once and turn once only
We think of the key, each in his prison
Thinking of the key, each confirms a prison
Only at nightfall, aetherial rumours   415
Revive for a moment a broken Coriolanus
DA
Damyata: The boat responded
Gaily, to the hand expert with sail and oar
The sea was calm, your heart would have responded   420
Gaily, when invited, beating obedient
To controlling hands

        I sat upon the shore
Fishing, with the arid plain behind me
Shall I at least set my lands in order?   425

London Bridge is falling down falling down falling down

Poi s'ascose nel foco che gli affina
Quando fiam ceu chelidon—O swallow swallow
Le Prince d'Aquitaine à la tour abolie
These fragments I have shored against my ruins   430
Why then Ile fit you. Hieronymo's mad againe.
Datta. Dayadhvam. Damyata.

     Shantih   shantih   shantih

NOTES

Not only the title, but the plan and a good deal of the incidental sym-
bolism of the poem were suggested by Miss Jessie L. Weston's book
on the Grail legend: From Ritual to Romance (Macmillan). Indeed, so
deeply am I indebted, Miss Weston's book will elucidate the difficul-
ties of the poem much better than my notes can do; and I recommend
it (apart from the great interest of the book itself) to any who think
such elucidation of the poem worth the trouble. To another work of
anthropology I am indebted in general, one which has influenced
our generation profoundly; I mean The Golden Bough; I have used
especially the two volumes Attis Adonis Osiris. Anyone who is ac-
quainted with these works will immediately recognise in the poem
certain references to vegetation ceremonies.

I. THE BURIAL OF THE DEAD

Line 20 Cf. Ezekiel II, i.

23. Cf. Ecclesiastes XII, v.

31. V. Tristan und Isolde, I, verses 5–8.

42. Id. III, verse 24.

46. I am not familiar with the exact constitution of the Tarot pack of
cards, from which I have obviously departed to suit my own conve-
nience. The Hanged Man, a member of the traditional pack, fits my
purpose in two ways: because he is associated in my mind with the
Hanged God of Frazer, and because I associate him with the hood-
ed figure in the passage of the disciples to Emmaus in Part V. The
Phoenician Sailor and the Merchant appear later; also the "crowds
of people," and Death by Water is executed in Part IV. The Man with
Three Staves (an authentic member of the Tarot pack) I associate,
quite arbitrarily, with the Fisher King himself.

60. Cf. Baudelaire:
"Fourmillante cité, cité pleine de rêves,
Où le spectre en plein jour raccroche le passant."

63. Cf. Inferno, III. 55–57:
          "si lunga tratta
di gente, ch'io non avrei mai creduto
che morte tanta n'avesse disfatta."

64. Cf. Inferno, IV. 25–27:
"Quivi, secondo che per ascoltare,
"non avea pianto, ma' che di sospiri,
"che l'aura eterna facevan tremare."

68. A phenomenon which I have often noticed.

74. Cf. the Dirge in Webster's White Devil.

76. V. Baudelaire, Preface to Fleurs du Mal.

II. A GAME OF CHESS

77. Cf. Antony and Cleopatra, II., ii. l. 190.

92. Laquearia. V. Aeneid, I, 726:
     dependent lychni laquearibus aureis
incensi, et noctem flammis funalia vincunt.

98. Sylvan scene. V. Milton, Paradise Lost, IV. 140.

99. V. Ovid, Metamorphoses, VI, Philomela.

100. Cf. Part III, l. 204.

115. Cf. Part III, l. 195.

118. Cf. Webster: "Is the wind in that door still?"

126. Cf. Part I, l. 37, 48.

138. Cf. the game of chess in Middleton's Women beware Women.

III. THE FIRE SERMON

176. V. Spenser, Prothalamion.

192. Cf. The Tempest, I, ii.

196. Cf. Day, Parliament of Bees:
"When of the sudden, listening, you shall hear,
"A noise of horns and hunting, which shall bring
"Actaeon to Diana in the spring,
"Where all shall see her naked skin…"

197. Cf. Marvell, To His Coy Mistress.

199. I do not know the origin of the ballad from which these lines are taken; it was reported to me from Sydney, Australia.

202. V. Verlaine, Parsifal.

210. The currants were quoted at a price "carriage and insurance free to London"; and the Bill of Lading, etc. were to be handed to the buyer upon payment of the sight draft.

218. Tiresias, although a mere spectator and not indeed a "character," is yet the most important personage in the poem, uniting all the rest. Just as the one-eyed merchant, seller of currants, melts into the Phoenician Sailor, and the latter is not wholly distinct from Ferdinand Prince of Naples, so all the women are one woman, and the two

sexes meet in Tiresias. What Tiresias sees, in fact, is the substance of the poem. The whole passage from Ovid is of great anthropological interest:

...Cum Iunone iocos et maior vestra profecto est
Quam, quae contingit maribus', dixisse, 'voluptas.'
Illa negat; placuit quae sit sententia docti
Quaerere Tiresiae: venus huic erat utraque nota.
Nam duo magnorum viridi coeuntia silva
Corpora serpentum baculi violaverat ictu
Deque viro factus, mirabile, femina septem
Egerat autumnos; octavo rursus eosdem
Vidit et 'est vestrae si tanta potentia plagae,'
Dixit 'ut auctoris sortem in contraria mutet,
Nunc quoque vos feriam!' percussis anguibus isdem
Forma prior rediit genetivaque venit imago.
Arbiter hic igitur sumptus de lite iocosa
Dicta Iovis firmat; gravius Saturnia iusto
Nec pro materia fertur doluisse suique
Iudicis aeterna damnavit lumina nocte,
At pater omnipotens (neque enim licet inrita cuiquam
Facta dei fecisse deo) pro lumine adempto
Scire futura dedit poenamque levavit honore.

221. This may not appear as exact as Sappho's lines, but I had in mind the "longshore" or "dory" fisherman, who returns at nightfall.

253. V. Goldsmith, the song in The Vicar of Wakefield.

257. V. The Tempest, as above.

264. The interior of St. Magnus Martyr is to my mind one of the finest among Wren's interiors. See The Proposed Demolition of Nineteen City Churches: (P. S. King & Son, Ltd.).

266. The Song of the (three) Thames-daughters begins here. From

line 292 to 306 inclusive they speak in turn. V. Götterdämmerung, III, i: The Rhinedaughters.

279. V. Froude, Elizabeth, Vol. I, ch. iv, letter of De Quadra to Philip of Spain:
"In the afternoon we were in a barge, watching the games on the river. (The queen) was alone with Lord Robert and myself on the poop, when they began to talk nonsense, and went so far that Lord Robert at last said, as I was on the spot there was no reason why they should not be married if the queen pleased."

293. Cf. Purgatorio, V. 133:
    "Ricorditi di me, che son la Pia;
    "Siena mi fe', disfecemi Maremma."

307. V. St. Augustine's Confessions: "to Carthage then I came, where a cauldron of unholy loves sang all about mine ears."

308. The complete text of the Buddha's Fire Sermon (which corresponds in importance to the Sermon on the Mount) from which these words are taken, will be found translated in the late Henry Clarke Warren's Buddhism in Translation (Harvard Oriental Series). Mr. Warren was one of the great pioneers of Buddhist studies in the occident.

309. From St. Augustine's Confessions again. The collocation of these two representatives of eastern and western asceticism, as the culmination of this part of the poem, is not an accident.

V. WHAT THE THUNDER SAID

In the first part of Part V three themes are employed: the journey to Emmaus, the approach to the Chapel Perilous (see Miss Weston's book), and the present decay of eastern Europe.

357. This is Turdus aonalaschkae pallasii, the hermit-thrush which I have heard in Quebec County. Chapman says (Handbook of Birds in Eastern North America) "it is most at home in secluded woodland and thickety retreats.... Its notes are not remarkable for variety or volume, but in purity and sweetness of tone and exquisite modulation they are unequaled." Its "water-dripping song" is justly celebrated.

360. The following lines were stimulated by the account of one of the Antarctic expeditions (I forget which, but I think one of Shackleton's): it was related that the party of explorers, at the extremity of their strength, had the constant delusion that there was one more member than could actually be counted.

366–76. Cf. Hermann Hesse, Blick ins Chaos: "Schon ist halb Europa, schon ist zumindest der halbe Osten Europas auf dem Wege zum Chaos, fährt betrunken im heiligem Wahn am Abgrund entlang und singt dazu, singt betrunken und hymnisch wie Dmitri Karamasoff sang. Ueber diese Lieder lacht der Bürger beleidigt, der Heilige und Seher hört sie mit Tränen."

401. "Datta, dayadhvam, damyata" (Give, sympathise, control). The fable of the meaning of the Thunder is found in the Brihadaranyaka—Upanishad, 5, 1. A translation is found in Deussen's Sechzig Upanishads des Veda, p. 489.

407. Cf. Webster, The White Devil, V, vi:
"...they'll remarry
Ere the worm pierce your winding-sheet, ere the spider
Make a thin curtain for your epitaphs."

411. Cf. Inferno, XXXIII, 46:
"ed io sentii chiavar l'uscio di sotto
all'orribile torre."
   Also F. H. Bradley, Appearance and Reality, p. 346.

"My external sensations are no less private to myself than are my thoughts or my feelings. In either case my experience falls within my own circle, a circle closed on the outside; and, with all its elements alike, every sphere is opaque to the others which surround it.... In brief, regarded as an existence which appears in a soul, the whole world for each is peculiar and private to that soul."

424. V. Weston, From Ritual to Romance; chapter on the Fisher King.

427. V. Purgatorio, XXVI, 148.
"'Ara vos prec, per aquella valor
'que vos guida al som de l'escalina,
'sovegna vos a temps de ma dolor.'
Poi s'ascose nel foco che gli affina."

428. V. Pervigilium Veneris. Cf. Philomela in Parts II and III.

429. V. Gerard de Nerval, Sonnet El Desdichado.

431. V. Kyd's Spanish Tragedy.

433. Shantih. Repeated as here, a formal ending to an Upanishad. "The Peace which passeth understanding" is a feeble translation of the content of this word.

The Love Song of J. Alfred Prufrock

S'io credesse che mia risposta fosse
A persona che mai tornasse al mondo,
Questa fiamma staria senza piu scosse.
Ma perciocche giammai di questo fondo
Non torno vivo alcun, s'i'odo il vero,
Senza tema d'infamia ti rispondo.

Let us go then, you and I,
When the evening is spread out against the sky
Like a patient etherized upon a table;
Let us go, through certain half-deserted streets,
The muttering retreats
Of restless nights in one-night cheap hotels
And sawdust restaurants with oyster-shells:
Streets that follow like a tedious argument
Of insidious intent
To lead you to an overwhelming question....
Oh, do not ask, "What is it?"
Let us go and make our visit.

In the room the women come and go
Talking of Michelangelo.

The yellow fog that rubs its back upon the window-panes,
The yellow smoke that rubs its muzzle on the window-panes
Licked its tongue into the corners of the evening,
Lingered upon the pools that stand in drains,
Let fall upon its back the soot that falls from chimneys,
Slipped by the terrace, made a sudden leap,
And seeing that it was a soft October night,
Curled once about the house, and fell asleep.

And indeed there will be time
For the yellow smoke that slides along the street,
Rubbing its back upon the window panes;
There will be time, there will be time
To prepare a face to meet the faces that you meet
There will be time to murder and create,
And time for all the works and days of hands
That lift and drop a question on your plate;
Time for you and time for me,
And time yet for a hundred indecisions,
And for a hundred visions and revisions,
Before the taking of a toast and tea.

In the room the women come and go
Talking of Michelangelo.

And indeed there will be time
To wonder, "Do I dare?" and, "Do I dare?"
Time to turn back and descend the stair,
With a bald spot in the middle of my hair--
(They will say: "How his hair is growing thin!")
My morning coat, my collar mounting firmly to the chin,
My necktie rich and modest, but asserted by a simple pin--
(They will say: "But how his arms and legs are thin!")
Do I dare
Disturb the universe?
In a minute there is time
For decisions and revisions which a minute will reverse.

For I have known them all already, known them all:
Have known the evenings, mornings, afternoons,
I have measured out my life with coffee spoons;
I know the voices dying with a dying fall
Beneath the music from a farther room.
            So how should I presume?

And I have known the eyes already, known them all--
The eyes that fix you in a formulated phrase,
And when I am formulated, sprawling on a pin,
When I am pinned and wriggling on the wall,
Then how should I begin
To spit out all the butt-ends of my days and ways?
                    And how should I presume?

And I have known the arms already, known them all--
Arms that are braceleted and white and bare
(But in the lamplight, downed with light brown hair!)
Is it perfume from a dress
That makes me so digress?
Arms that lie along a table, or wrap about a shawl.
                    And should I then presume?
                    And how should I begin?

Shall I say, I have gone at dusk through narrow streets
And watched the smoke that rises from the pipes
Of lonely men in shirt-sleeves, leaning out of windows?

I should have been a pair of ragged claws
Scuttling across the floors of silent seas.

And the afternoon, the evening, sleeps so peacefully!
Smoothed by long fingers,
Asleep... tired... or it malingers.
Stretched on the floor, here beside you and me.
Should I, after tea and cakes and ices,
Have the strength to force the moment to its crisis?
But though I have wept and fasted, wept and prayed,
Though I have seen my head (grown slightly bald) brought in upon
a platter,
I am no prophet--and here's no great matter;
I have seen the moment of my greatness flicker,

And I have seen the eternal Footman hold my coat, and snicker,
And in short, I was afraid.

And would it have been worth it, after all,
After the cups, the marmalade, the tea,
Among the porcelain, among some talk of you and me,
Would it have been worth while,
To have bitten off the matter with a smile,
To have squeezed the universe into a ball
To roll it toward some overwhelming question,
To say: "I am Lazarus, come from the dead,
Come back to tell you all, I shall tell you all"--
If one, settling a pillow by her head,
        Should say: "That is not what I meant at all;
        That is not it, at all."

And would it have been worth it, after all,
Would it have been worth while,
After the sunsets and the dooryards and the sprinkled streets,
After the novels, after the teacups, after the skirts that trail along the
  floor--
And this, and so much more?--
It is impossible to say just what I mean!
But as if a magic lantern threw the nerves in patterns on a screen:
Would it have been worth while
If one, settling a pillow or throwing off a shawl,
And turning toward the window, should say:
        "That is not it at all,
        That is not what I meant, at all."

No! I am not Prince Hamlet, nor was meant to be;
Am an attendant lord, one that will do
To swell a progress, start a scene or two,
Advise the prince; no doubt, an easy tool,
Deferential, glad to be of use,

Politic, cautious, and meticulous;
Full of high sentence, but a bit obtuse;
At times, indeed, almost ridiculous--
Almost, at times, the Fool.

I grow old... I grow old...
I shall wear the bottoms of my trousers rolled.

Shall I part my hair behind? Do I dare to eat a peach?
I shall wear white flannel trousers, and walk upon the beach.
I have heard the mermaids singing, each to each.

I do not think that they will sing to me.

I have seen them riding seaward on the waves
Combing the white hair of the waves blown back
When the wind blows the water white and black.

We have lingered in the chambers of the sea
By sea-girls wreathed with seaweed red and brown
Till human voices wake us, and we drown.

Portrait of a Lady

Thou hast committed--
Fornication: but that was in another country
And besides, the wench is dead.
                              The Jew of Malta.

I

Among the smoke and fog of a December afternoon
You have the scene arrange itself--as it will seem to do--
With "I have saved this afternoon for you";
And four wax candles in the darkened room,
Four rings of light upon the ceiling overhead,
An atmosphere of Juliet's tomb
Prepared for all the things to be said, or left unsaid.
We have been, let us say, to hear the latest Pole
Transmit the Preludes, through his hair and finger-tips.
"So intimate, this Chopin, that I think his soul
Should be resurrected only among friends
Some two or three, who will not touch the bloom
That is rubbed and questioned in the concert room."
--And so the conversation slips
Among velleities and carefully caught regrets
Through attenuated tones of violins
Mingled with remote cornets
And begins.

"You do not know how much they mean to me, my friends,
And how, how rare and strange it is, to find
In a life composed so much, so much of odds and ends,
(For indeed I do not love it... you knew? you are not blind!
How keen you are!)

To find a friend who has these qualities,
Who has, and gives
Those qualities upon which friendship lives.
How much it means that I say this to you--
Without these friendships--life, what cauchemar!"

Among the windings of the violins
And the ariettes
Of cracked cornets
Inside my brain a dull tom-tom begins
Absurdly hammering a prelude of its own,
Capricious monotone
That is at least one definite "false note."
--Let us take the air, in a tobacco trance,
Admire the monuments
Discuss the late events,
Correct our watches by the public clocks.
Then sit for half an hour and drink our bocks.

II

Now that lilacs are in bloom
She has a bowl of lilacs in her room
And twists one in her fingers while she talks.
"Ah, my friend, you do not know, you do not know
What life is, you should hold it in your hands";
(Slowly twisting the lilac stalks)
"You let it flow from you, you let it flow,
And youth is cruel, and has no remorse
And smiles at situations which it cannot see."
I smile, of course,
And go on drinking tea.
"Yet with these April sunsets, that somehow recall
My buried life, and Paris in the Spring,

I feel immeasurably at peace, and find the world
To be wonderful and youthful, after all."

The voice returns like the insistent out-of-tune
Of a broken violin on an August afternoon:
"I am always sure that you understand
My feelings, always sure that you feel,
Sure that across the gulf you reach your hand.

You are invulnerable, you have no Achilles' heel.
You will go on, and when you have prevailed
You can say: at this point many a one has failed.

But what have I, but what have I, my friend,
To give you, what can you receive from me?
Only the friendship and the sympathy
Of one about to reach her journey's end.

I shall sit here, serving tea to friends...."

I take my hat: how can I make a cowardly amends
For what she has said to me?
You will see me any morning in the park
Reading the comics and the sporting page.
Particularly I remark An English countess goes upon the stage.
A Greek was murdered at a Polish dance,
Another bank defaulter has confessed.
I keep my countenance, I remain self-possessed
Except when a street piano, mechanical and tired
Reiterates some worn-out common song
With the smell of hyacinths across the garden
Recalling things that other people have desired.
Are these ideas right or wrong?

III

The October night comes down; returning as before
Except for a slight sensation of being ill at ease
I mount the stairs and turn the handle of the door
And feel as if I had mounted on my hands and knees.

"And so you are going abroad; and when do you return?
But that's a useless question.
You hardly know when you are coming back,
You will find so much to learn."
My smile falls heavily among the bric-à-brac.

"Perhaps you can write to me."
My self-possession flares up for a second;
This is as I had reckoned.

"I have been wondering frequently of late
(But our beginnings never know our ends!)
Why we have not developed into friends."
I feel like one who smiles, and turning shall remark
Suddenly, his expression in a glass.
My self-possession gutters; we are really in the dark.

"For everybody said so, all our friends,
They all were sure our feelings would relate
So closely! I myself can hardly understand.
We must leave it now to fate.
You will write, at any rate.
Perhaps it is not too late.
I shall sit here, serving tea to friends."

And I must borrow every changing shape
To find expression... dance, dance
Like a dancing bear,

Cry like a parrot, chatter like an ape.
Let us take the air, in a tobacco trance--
Well! and what if she should die some afternoon,
Afternoon grey and smoky, evening yellow and rose;
Should die and leave me sitting pen in hand
With the smoke coming down above the housetops;
Doubtful, for quite a while
Not knowing what to feel or if I understand
Or whether wise or foolish, tardy or too soon...
Would she not have the advantage, after all?
This music is successful with a "dying fall"
Now that we talk of dying--
And should I have the right to smile?

Preludes

I

The winter evening settles down
With smell of steaks in passageways.
Six o'clock.
The burnt-out ends of smoky days.
And now a gusty shower wraps
The grimy scraps
Of withered leaves about your feet
And newspapers from vacant lots;
The showers beat
On broken blinds and chimney-pots,
And at the corner of the street
A lonely cab-horse steams and stamps.

And then the lighting of the lamps.

II

The morning comes to consciousness
Of faint stale smells of beer
From the sawdust-trampled street
With all its muddy feet that press
To early coffee-stands.

With the other masquerades
That time resumes,
One thinks of all the hands
That are raising dingy shades
In a thousand furnished rooms.

III

You tossed a blanket from the bed,
You lay upon your back, and waited;
You dozed, and watched the night revealing
The thousand sordid images
Of which your soul was constituted;
They flickered against the ceiling.
And when all the world came back
And the light crept up between the shutters,
And you heard the sparrows in the gutters,
You had such a vision of the street
As the street hardly understands;
Sitting along the bed's edge, where
You curled the papers from your hair,
Or clasped the yellow soles of feet
In the palms of both soiled hands.

IV

His soul stretched tight across the skies
That fade behind a city block,
Or trampled by insistent feet
At four and five and six o'clock;
And short square fingers stuffing pipes,
And evening newspapers, and eyes
Assured of certain certainties,
The conscience of a blackened street
Impatient to assume the world.

I am moved by fancies that are curled
Around these images, and cling:
The notion of some infinitely gentle
Infinitely suffering thing.

Wipe your hand across your mouth, and laugh;
The worlds revolve like ancient women
Gathering fuel in vacant lots.

Rhapsody on a Windy Night

Twelve o'clock.
Along the reaches of the street
Held in a lunar synthesis,
Whispering lunar incantations
Disolve the floors of memory
And all its clear relations,
Its divisions and precisions,
Every street lamp that I pass
Beats like a fatalistic drum,
And through the spaces of the dark
Midnight shakes the memory
As a madman shakes a dead geranium.

Half-past one,
The street lamp sputtered,
The street lamp muttered,
The street lamp said,
"Regard that woman
Who hesitates toward you in the light of the door
Which opens on her like a grin.
You see the border of her dress
Is torn and stained with sand,
And you see the corner of her eye
Twists like a crooked pin."

The memory throws up high and dry
A crowd of twisted things;
A twisted branch upon the beach
Eaten smooth, and polished
As if the world gave up
The secret of its skeleton,
Stiff and white.
A broken spring in a factory yard,

Rust that clings to the form that the strength has left
Hard and curled and ready to snap.

Half-past two,
The street-lamp said,
"Remark the cat which flattens itself in the gutter,
Slips out its tongue
And devours a morsel of rancid butter."
So the hand of the child, automatic,
Slipped out and pocketed a toy that was running along
the quay.
I could see nothing behind that child's eye.
I have seen eyes in the street
Trying to peer through lighted shutters,
And a crab one afternoon in a pool,
An old crab with barnacles on his back,
Gripped the end of a stick which I held him.

Half-past three,
The lamp sputtered,
The lamp muttered in the dark.

The lamp hummed:
"Regard the moon,
La lune ne garde aucune rancune,
She winks a feeble eye,
She smiles into corners.
She smooths the hair of the grass.
The moon has lost her memory.
A washed-out smallpox cracks her face,
Her hand twists a paper rose,
That smells of dust and old Cologne,
She is alone With all the old nocturnal smells
That cross and cross across her brain.
The reminiscence comes

Of sunless dry geraniums
And dust in crevices,
Smells of chestnuts in the streets
And female smells in shuttered rooms
And cigarettes in corridors
And cocktail smells in bars."

The lamp said,
"Four o'clock,
Here is the number on the door.
Memory!
You have the key,
The little lamp spreads a ring on the stair,
Mount.
The bed is open; the tooth-brush hangs on the wall,
Put your shoes at the door, sleep, prepare for life."

The last twist of the knife.

Gerontion

Thou hast nor youth nor age
But as it were an after dinner sleep
Dreaming of both.

Here I am, an old man in a dry month,
Being read to by a boy, waiting for rain.
I was neither at the hot gates
Nor fought in the warm rain
Nor knee deep in the salt marsh, heaving a cutlass,
Bitten by flies, fought.
My house is a decayed house,
And the jew squats on the window sill, the owner,
Spawned in some estaminet of Antwerp,
Blistered in Brussels, patched and peeled in London.
The goat coughs at night in the field overhead;
Rocks, moss, stonecrop, iron, merds.
The woman keeps the kitchen, makes tea,
Sneezes at evening, poking the peevish gutter.
                    I an old man,
A dull head among windy spaces.

Signs are taken for wonders. "We would see a sign":
The word within a word, unable to speak a word,
Swaddled with darkness. In the juvescence of the year
Came Christ the tiger

In depraved May, dogwood and chestnut, flowering Judas,
To be eaten, to be divided, to be drunk
Among whispers; by Mr. Silvero
With caressing hands, at Limoges
Who walked all night in the next room;

By Hakagawa, bowing among the Titians;
By Madame de Tornquist, in the dark room
Shifting the candles; Fraulein von Kulp
Who turned in the hall, one hand on the door. Vacant shuttles
Weave the wind. I have no ghosts,
An old man in a draughty house
Under a windy knob.

After such knowledge, what forgiveness? Think now
History has many cunning passages, contrived corridors
And issues, deceives with whispering ambitions,
Guides us by vanities. Think now
She gives when our attention is distracted
And what she gives, gives with such supple confusions
That the giving famishes the craving. Gives too late
What's not believed in, or if still believed,
In memory only, reconsidered passion. Gives too soon
Into weak hands, what's thought can be dispensed with
Till the refusal propagates a fear. Think
Neither fear nor courage saves us. Unnatural vices
Are fathered by our heroism. Virtues
Are forced upon us by our impudent crimes.
These tears are shaken from the wrath-bearing tree.

The tiger springs in the new year. Us he devours. Think at last
We have not reached conclusion, when I
Stiffen in a rented house. Think at last
I have not made this show purposelessly
And it is not by any concitation
Of the backward devils.
I would meet you upon this honestly.
I that was near your heart was removed therefrom
To lose beauty in terror, terror in inquisition.
I have lost my passion: why should I need to keep it
Since what is kept must be adulterated?

I have lost my sight, smell, hearing, taste and touch:
How should I use it for your closer contact?

These with a thousand small deliberations
Protract the profit of their chilled delirium,
Excite the membrane, when the sense has cooled,
With pungent sauces, multiply variety
In a wilderness of mirrors. What will the spider do,
Suspend its operations, will the weevil
Delay? De Bailhache, Fresca, Mrs. Cammel, whirled
Beyond the circuit of the shuddering Bear
In fractured atoms. Gull against the wind, in the windy straits
Of Belle Isle, or running on the Horn,
White feathers in the snow, the Gulf claims,
And an old man driven by the Trades
To a sleepy corner.

               Tenants of the house,
Thoughts of a dry brain in a dry season.

Burbank with a Baedeker:
Bleistein with a Cigar

Tra-la-la-la-la-la-laire—nil nisi divinum stabile est; caetera fumus—the gondola stopped, the old palace was there, how charming its grey and pink—goats and monkeys, with such hair too!—so the countess passed on until she came through the little park, where Niobe presented her with a cabinet, and so departed.

BURBANK crossed a little bridge
    Descending at a small hotel;
Princess Volupine arrived,
    They were together, and he fell.

Defunctive music under sea
    Passed seaward with the passing bell
Slowly: the God Hercules
    Had left him, that had loved him well.

The horses, under the axletree
    Beat up the dawn from Istria
With even feet. Her shuttered barge
    Burned on the water all the day.

But this or such was Bleistein's way:
    A saggy bending of the knees
And elbows, with the palms turned out,
    Chicago Semite Viennese.

A lustreless protrusive eye
    Stares from the protozoic slime
At a perspective of Canaletto.
    The smoky candle end of time

Declines. On the Rialto once.
            The rats are underneath the piles.
The jew is underneath the lot.
            Money in furs. The boatman smiles,

Princess Volupine extends
            A meagre, blue-nailed, phthisic hand
To climb the waterstair. Lights, lights,
            She entertains Sir Ferdinand

Klein. Who clipped the lion's wings
            And flea'd his rump and pared his claws?
Thought Burbank, meditating on
            Time's ruins, and the seven laws.

Sweeney Erect

And the trees about me,
Let them be dry and leafless; let the rocks
Groan with continual surges; and behind me
Make all a desolation. Look, look, wenches!

Paint me a cavernous waste shore
Cast in the unstilted Cyclades,
Paint me the bold anfractuous rocks
Faced by the snarled and yelping seas.

Display me Aeolus above
Reviewing the insurgent gales
Which tangle Ariadne's hair
And swell with haste the perjured sails.

Morning stirs the feet and hands
(Nausicaa and Polypheme),
Gesture of orang-outang
Rises from the sheets in steam.

This withered root of knots of hair
Slitted below and gashed with eyes,
This oval O cropped out with teeth:
The sickle motion from the thighs

Jackknifes upward at the knees
Then straightens out from heel to hip
Pushing the framework of the bed
And clawing at the pillow slip.

Sweeney addressed full length to shave

Broadbottomed, pink from nape to base,
Knows the female temperament
And wipes the suds around his face.

(The lengthened shadow of a man
Is history, said Emerson
Who had not seen the silhouette
Of Sweeney straddled in the sun).

Tests the razor on his leg
Waiting until the shriek subsides.
The epileptic on the bed
Curves backward, clutching at her sides.

The ladies of the corridor
Find themselves involved, disgraced,
Call witness to their principles
And deprecate the lack of taste

Observing that hysteria
Might easily be misunderstood;
Mrs. Turner intimates
It does the house no sort of good.

But Doris, towelled from the bath,
Enters padding on broad feet,
Bringing sal volatile
And a glass of brandy neat.

A Cooking Egg

En l'an trentiesme de mon aage
Que toutes mes hontes j'ay beues...

Pipit sate upright in her chair
Some distance from where I was sitting;
   Views of the Oxford Colleges
Lay on the table, with the knitting.

Daguerreotypes and silhouettes,
Her grandfather and great great aunts,
   Supported on the mantelpiece
An Invitation to the Dance.

I shall not want Honour in Heaven
For I shall meet Sir Philip Sidney
   And have talk with Coriolanus
And other heroes of that kidney.

I shall not want Capital in Heaven
For I shall meet Sir Alfred Mond:
   We two shall lie together, lapt
In a five per cent Exchequer Bond.

I shall not want Society in Heaven,
Lucretia Borgia shall be my Bride;
   Her anecdotes will be more amusing
Than Pipit's experience could provide.

I shall not want Pipit in Heaven:
Madame Blavatsky will instruct me
   In the Seven Sacred Trances;
Piccarda de Donati will conduct me.

But where is the penny world I bought
To eat with Pipit behind the screen?
The red-eyed scavengers are creeping
From Kentish Town and Golder's Green;

Where are the eagles and the trumpets?

Buried beneath some snow-deep Alps.
Over buttered scones and crumpets
Weeping, weeping multitudes
Droop in a hundred A.B.C.'s

The Hippopotamus

Similiter et omnes revereantur Diaconos, ut
mandatum Jesu Christi; et Episcopum, ut Jesum
Christum, existentem filium Patris; Presbyteros
autem, ut concilium Dei et conjunctionem
Apostolorum. Sine his Ecclesia non vocatur; de
quibus suadeo vos sic habeo.

S. Ignatii Ad Trallianos

And when this epistle is read among you, cause
that it be read also in the church of the Laodiceans.

The broad-backed hippopotamus
Rests on his belly in the mud;
Although he seems so firm to us
He is merely flesh and blood.

Flesh-and-blood is weak and frail,
Susceptible to nervous shock;
While the True Church can never fail
For it is based upon a rock.

The hippo's feeble steps may err
In compassing material ends,
While the True Church need never stir
To gather in its dividends.

The 'potamus can never reach
The mango on the mango-tree;
But fruits of pomegranate and peach
Refresh the Church from over sea.

At mating time the hippo's voice

Betrays inflexions hoarse and odd,
But every week we hear rejoice
The Church, at being one with God.

The hippopotamus's day
Is passed in sleep; at night he hunts;
God works in a mysterious way-
The Church can sleep and feed at once.

I saw the 'potamus take wing
Ascending from the damp savannas,
And quiring angels round him sing
The praise of God, in loud hosannas.

Blood of the Lamb shall wash him clean
And him shall heavenly arms enfold,
Among the saints he shall be seen
Performing on a harp of gold.

He shall be washed as white as snow,
By all the martyr'd virgins kist,
While the True Church remains below
Wrapt in the old miasmal mist.

Mr. Eliot's Sunday Morning Service

Look, look, master, here comes two religious caterpillars.

Jew of Malta

POLYPHILOPROGENITIVE
The sapient sutlers of the Lord
Drift across the window-panes.
In the beginning was the Word.

In the beginning was the Word.
Superfetation of ,
And at the mensual turn of time
Produced enervate Origen.

A painter of the Umbrian school
Designed upon a gesso ground
The nimbus of the Baptized God.
The wilderness is cracked and browned

But through the water pale and thin
Still shine the unoffending feet
And there above the painter set
The Father and the Paraclete.
. . . . . .
The sable presbyters approach
The avenue of penitence;
The young are red and pustular
Clutching piaculative pence.

Under the penitential gates
Sustained by staring Seraphim
Where the souls of the devout
Burn invisible and dim.

Along the garden-wall the bees
With hairy bellies pass between
The staminate and pistilate,
Blest office of the epicene.

Sweeney shifts from ham to ham
Stirring the water in his bath.
The masters of the subtle schools
Are controversial, polymath.

Sweeney Among the Nightingales

ὤμοι, πέπληγμαι καιρίαν πληγὴν ἔσω.

Apeneck Sweeney spreads his knees
Letting his arms hang down to laugh,
The zebra stripes along his jaw
Swelling to maculate giraffe.

The circles of the stormy moon
Slide westward toward the River Plate,
Death and the Raven drift above
And Sweeney guards the hornèd gate.

Gloomy Orion and the Dog
Are veiled; and hushed the shrunken seas;
The person in the Spanish cape
Tries to sit on Sweeney›s knees

Slips and pulls the table cloth
Overturns a coffee-cup,
Reorganized upon the floor
She yawns and draws a stocking up;

The silent man in mocha brown
Sprawls at the window-sill and gapes;
The waiter brings in oranges
Bananas figs and hothouse grapes;

The silent vertebrate in brown
Contracts and concentrates, withdraws;
Rachel née Rabinovitch
Tears at the grapes with murderous paws;

She and the lady in the cape
Are suspect, thought to be in league;
Therefore the man with heavy eyes
Declines the gambit, shows fatigue,

Leaves the room and reappears
Outside the window, leaning in,
Branches of wisteria
Circumscribe a golden grin;

The host with someone indistinct
Converses at the door apart,
The nightingales are singing near
The Convent of the Sacred Heart,

And sang within the bloody wood
When Agamemnon cried aloud,
And let their liquid droppings fall
To stain the stiff dishonoured shroud.

The Hollow Men

Mistah Kurtz-he dead
                              A penny for the Old Guy

I

We are the hollow men
We are the stuffed men
Leaning together
Headpiece filled with straw. Alas!
Our dried voices, when
We whisper together
Are quiet and meaningless
As wind in dry grass
Or rats' feet over broken glass
In our dry cellar

Shape without form, shade without colour,
Paralysed force, gesture without motion;

Those who have crossed
With direct eyes, to death's other Kingdom
Remember us-if at all-not as lost
Violent souls, but only
As the hollow men
The stuffed men.

II

Eyes I dare not meet in dreams
In death's dream kingdom

These do not appear:
There, the eyes are
Sunlight on a broken column
There, is a tree swinging
And voices are
In the wind's singing
More distant and more solemn
Than a fading star.

Let me be no nearer
In death's dream kingdom
Let me also wear
Such deliberate disguises
Rat's coat, crowskin, crossed staves
In a field
Behaving as the wind behaves
No nearer-

Not that final meeting
In the twilight kingdom

III

This is the dead land
This is cactus land
Here the stone images
Are raised, here they receive
The supplication of a dead man's hand
Under the twinkle of a fading star.

Is it like this
In death's other kingdom
Waking alone
At the hour when we are

Trembling with tenderness
Lips that would kiss
Form prayers to broken stone.

IV

The eyes are not here
There are no eyes here
In this valley of dying stars
In this hollow valley
This broken jaw of our lost kingdoms

In this last of meeting places
We grope together
And avoid speech
Gathered on this beach of the tumid river

Sightless, unless
The eyes reappear
As the perpetual star
Multifoliate rose
Of death's twilight kingdom
The hope only
Of empty men.

V

Here we go round the prickly pear
Prickly pear prickly pear
Here we go round the prickly pear
At five o'clock in the morning.

Between the idea

And the reality
Between the motion
And the act
Falls the Shadow
 For Thine is the Kingdom

Between the conception
And the creation
Between the emotion
And the response
Falls the Shadow
 Life is very long

Between the desire
And the spasm
Between the potency
And the existence
Between the essence
And the descent
Falls the Shadow
 For Thine is the Kingdom

For Thine is
Life is
For Thine is the

This is the way the world ends
This is the way the world ends
This is the way the world ends
Not with a bang but a whimper.

Journey Of The Magi

'A cold coming we had of it,
Just the worst time of the year
For a journey, and such a long journey:
The ways deep and the weather sharp,
The very dead of winter.'
And the camels galled, sorefooted, refractory,
Lying down in the melting snow.
There were times we regretted
The summer palaces on slopes, the terraces,
And the silken girls bringing sherbet.
Then the camel men cursing and grumbling
and running away, and wanting their liquor and women,
And the night-fires going out, and the lack of shelters,
And the cities hostile and the towns unfriendly
And the villages dirty and charging high prices:
A hard time we had of it.
At the end we preferred to travel all night,
Sleeping in snatches,
With the voices singing in our ears, saying
That this was all folly.

Then at dawn we came down to a temperate valley,
Wet, below the snow line, smelling of vegetation;
With a running stream and a water-mill beating the darkness,
And three trees on the low sky,
And an old white horse galloped away in the meadow.
Then we came to a tavern with vine-leaves over the lintel,
Six hands at an open door dicing for pieces of silver,
And feet kicking the empty wine-skins.
But there was no information, and so we continued
And arriving at evening, not a moment too soon
Finding the place; it was (you might say) satisfactory.

All this was a long time ago, I remember,
And I would do it again, but set down
This set down
This: were we led all that way for
Birth or Death? There was a Birth, certainly
We had evidence and no doubt. I had seen birth and death,
But had thought they were different; this Birth was
Hard and bitter agony for us, like Death, our death.
We returned to our places, these Kingdoms,
But no longer at ease here, in the old dispensation,
With an alien people clutching their gods.
I should be glad of another death.

A Song For Simeon

Lord, they Roman hyacinths are blooming in bowls and
The winder sun creeps by the snow hills;
The stubborn season has made stand.
My life is light, waiting for the death wind,
Like a feather on the back of my hand.
Dust in sunlight and memory in corners
Wait for the wind that chills towards the dead land.

Grant us they peace.
I have walked many years in this city,
Kept faith and fast, provided for the poor,
have given and taken honour and ease.
There went never any rejected from my door.
Who shall remember my house, where shall live my children's
children?
When the time of sorrow is come?
They will take to the goat's path, and the fox's home,
Fleeing from foreign faces and the foreign swords.

Before the time of cords and scourges and lamentation
Grant us thy peace.
Before the stations of the mountain of desolation,
Before the certain hour of maternal sorrow,
Now at this birth season of decease,
Let the Infant, the still unspeaking and unspoken Word,
Grant Israel's consolation
To one who has eighty years and no to-morrow.

According to thy word.
They shall praise Thee and suffer in every generation
With glory and derision,
Light upon light, mounting the saints' stair.

Not for me the martyrdom, the ecstasy of thought and prayer,
Not for me the ultimate vision.
Grant me thy peace.
(And a sword shall pierce thy heart,
Thine also).
I am tired with my own life and the lives of those after me,
I am dying in my own death and the deaths of those after me.
Let they servant depart,
Having seen thy salvation.

Animula

'Issues from the hand of God, the simple soul'
To a flat world of changing lights and noise,
To light, dark, dry or damp, chilly or warm;
Moving between the legs of tables and of chairs,
Rising or falling, grasping at kisses and toys,
Advancing boldly, sudden to take alarm,
Retreating to the corner of arm and knee,
Eager to be reassured, taking pleasure
In the fragrant brilliance of the Christmas tree,
Pleasure in the wind, the sunlight and the sea;
Studies the sunlit pattern on the floor
And running stags around a silver tray;
Confounds the actual and the fanciful,
Content with playing-cards and kings and queens,
What the fairies do and what the servants say.
The heavy burden of the growing soul
Perplexes and offends more, day by day;
Week by week, offends and perplexes more
With the imperatives of 'is and seems'
And may and may not, desire and control.
The pain of living and the drug of dreams
Curl up the small soul in the window seat
Behind the Encyclopædia Britannica.
Issues from the hand of time the simple soul
Irresolute and selfish, misshapen, lame,
Unable to fare forward or retreat,
Fearing the warm reality, the offered good,
Denying the importunity of the blood,
Shadow of its own shadows, spectre in its own gloom,
Leaving disordered papers in a dusty room;
Living first in the silence after the viaticum.

Pray for Guiterriez, avid of speed and power,
For Boudin, blown to pieces,
For this one who made a great fortune,
And that one who went his own way.
Pray for Floret, by the boarhound slain between the yew trees,
Pray for us now and at the hour of our birth.

Marina

Quis hic locus, quae regio, quae mundi plaga?

What seas what shores what grey rocks and what islands
What water lapping the bow
And scent of pine and the woodthrush singing through the fog
What images return
O my daughter.

Those who sharpen the tooth of the dog, meaning
Death
Those who glitter with the glory of the hummingbird, meaning
Death
Those who sit in the stye of contentment, meaning
Death
Those who suffer the ecstasy of the animals, meaning
Death

Are become unsubstantial, reduced by a wind,
A breath of pine, and the woodsong fog
By this grace dissolved in place

What is this face, less clear and clearer
The pulse in the arm, less strong and stronger —
Given or lent? more distant than stars and nearer than the eye
Whispers and small laughter between leaves and hurrying feet
Under sleep, where all the waters meet.

Bowsprit cracked with ice and paint cracked with heat.
I made this, I have forgotten
And remember.
The rigging weak and the canvas rotten
Between one June and another September.

Made this unknowing, half conscious, unknown, my own.
The garboard strake leaks, the seams need caulking.
This form, this face, this life
Living to live in a world of time beyond me; let me
Resign my life for this life, my speech for that unspoken,
The awakened, lips parted, the hope, the new ships.
What seas what shores what granite islands towards my timbers
And woodthrush calling through the fog
My daughter.

Black Eagle Books

www.blackeaglebooks.org
info@blackeaglebooks.org

Black Eagle Books, an independent publisher, was founded
as a nonprofit organization in April, 2019. It is our mission
to connect and engage the Indian diaspora and the world at
large with the best of works of world literature published on
a collaborative platform, with special emphasis on
foregrounding Contemporary Classics and New Writing.

Milton Keynes UK
Ingram Content Group UK Ltd.
UKHW012146040124
435404UK00004BA/135